# Minerals

by Melissa Stewart

Heinemann Library
CHICAGO, ILLINOIS

© 2002 Reed Educational & Professional Publishing
Published by Heinemann Library,
an imprint of Reed Educational & Professional Publishing,
Chicago, Illinois
Customer Service 888-454-2279
Visit our website at www.heinemannlibrary.com

Designed by Ox and Company

An Editorial Directions book

Printed in Hong Kong

06 05 04 03 02
10 9 8 7 6 5 4 3 2 1

**Library of Congress Cataloging-in-Publication Data**
Stewart, Melissa.
    Minerals / Melissa Stewart.
        p. cm.—(Rocks and minerals)
Includes bibliographical references and index.
Summary: Provides an overview of minerals including how they were formed,
their characteristics, history, common kinds of minerals and their uses, and
amazing mineral facts.
    ISBN: 1-58810-258-0 (HC), 1-4034-0094-6 (Pbk.)
    1. Minerals—Juvenile literature. [1. Minerals.] I. Title.
    QE365.2 .S74 2002
    549—dc21                                        2001002759

**Acknowledgments**
The author and publishers are grateful to the following for permission to reproduce copyright material:

Photographs ©: Cover, Tom O'Brien/International Stock; p. 4, Tom & Therisa Stack/Tom Stack & Associates; p. 5, Steve
Berman/Liaison International/Hulton Archive; p. 6, Mark A. Schneider/Visuals Unlimited, Inc.; p. 7, Brian Parker/Tom Stack
& Associates; p. 8, M. Bernsau/The Image Works; p. 9, Cameramann International, Ltd.; p. 10, Stuart Cohen/The Image
Works; p. 11, Grace Davies Photography; p. 13, G. Brad Lewis/Liaison International/Hulton Archive; p. 14, James L.
Amos/Corbis; p. 15, B. Daemmrich/The Image Works; p. 16, E. Sander/Gamma Liaison/Hulton Archive; p. 17, Tom & Therisa
Stack/Tom Stack & Associates; p. 18,  David Johnson/Reed Consumer Books, Ltd.; p. 19, Mark A. Schneider/Visuals
Unlimited, Inc.; p. 20, Grace Davies Photography; p. 21, José Manuel Sanchis Calvete/Corbis; p. 22, Margot Granitsas/The
Image Works; p. 23, T.A. Natarajan/DPA/The Image Works; p. 24, NASA/The Image Works; p. 25, Grace Davies
Photography; p. 26, Francis G. Mayer/Corbis; p. 27, DeRichemond/The Image Works; p. 28, Arthur Gurmankin/Visuals
Unlimited, Inc.; p. 29, Grace Davies Photography.

Some words are shown in bold, **like this.** You can find out what they mean by looking in the glossary.

# Contents

What Is a Mineral? . . . . . . . . . . . . . . . . . . . . . 4

Inside a Mineral . . . . . . . . . . . . . . . . . . . . . . . 6

The Most Common Minerals . . . . . . . . . . . . . . 8

Is That a Mineral? . . . . . . . . . . . . . . . . . . . . . 10

Below the Surface . . . . . . . . . . . . . . . . . . . . . 12

What Mineral Is That? . . . . . . . . . . . . . . . . . . 14

Taking a Good, Long Look . . . . . . . . . . . . . . . 16

Let's Get Physical . . . . . . . . . . . . . . . . . . . . . . 18

How Hard Is That Mineral? . . . . . . . . . . . . . . 20

Digging Up Minerals . . . . . . . . . . . . . . . . . . . 22

How People Use Minerals . . . . . . . . . . . . . . . . 24

Amazing Minerals . . . . . . . . . . . . . . . . . . . . . 26

Be a Mineral Collector . . . . . . . . . . . . . . . . . . 28

*Glossary* . . . . . . . . . . . . . . . . . . . . . . . . . . . . . *30*

*To Find Out More* . . . . . . . . . . . . . . . . . . . . . *31*

*Index* . . . . . . . . . . . . . . . . . . . . . . . . . . . . . . . *32*

# What Is a Mineral?

Gold is a mineral and a metal. Flakes of gold can sometimes be found in rivers and streams.

When you hear people use the word "mineral," do you know exactly what they mean? You probably know that minerals are related to rocks. You might also know that they are sometimes dug out of mines. But it can be hard to explain exactly what a mineral is.

A mineral is a natural solid material that is not alive. Gold, diamond, quartz, talc, and calcite are all minerals. More importantly, a mineral always has the same chemical makeup and the same structure, no matter where you find it.

What does this mean? Think about all the different kinds of chocolate chip cookies you have eaten in your life. Some were probably thin and flat. Others

**DID YOU KNOW?**

There are about 3,000 kinds of minerals on Earth, but many are very rare. A group of about 100 minerals combine in different ways to make most of the rocks we know.

might have been thick and puffy. Maybe a few had nuts or peanut butter chips mixed in. When you make cookies, you follow a recipe so that they will turn out just the way you like them. But even if you and a friend use the same exact recipe, your cookies may turn out differently. If you and your friend use different brands of margarine or different-sized eggs, your cookie batter will not be exactly the same. As a result, your cookies may have different structures. Your friend's cookies may be small and puffy, while your own cookies are large and flat.

### MINERAL MIXTURES

Different kinds of minerals join together to form rocks. Some rocks contain just one type of mineral, but most contain between two and ten minerals. Granite (above) is a rock that usually contains the minerals quartz, feldspar, and mica. Marble is a rock made mostly of the minerals calcite and dolomite.

Minerals are not like cookies. Two samples of gold always have the same mix of ingredients, so they always look the same—both inside and outside.

# Inside a Mineral

Just as a rock is a mixture of minerals, a mineral is a mixture of **elements.** An element is a substance that contains only one kind of **atom.** Scientists have identified more than 100 different elements on Earth, but 99 percent of all minerals are made up of just eight elements. These popular elements have familiar names—oxygen, silicon, aluminum, iron, magnesium, calcium, potassium, and sodium.

Quartz is one of the most common minerals on Earth. It contains just two elements—silicon and oxygen. The atoms in quartz are always arranged in the same way. Each atom of silicon attaches to, or bonds with, two atoms of oxygen.

Pure quartz is colorless. But when a few iron atoms mix with silicon and oxygen atoms, a purple mineral called amethyst forms. When a few

## ALL ABOUT ATOMS

Every object in the universe that has mass and takes up space is known as **matter.** The book you're holding in your hand is matter. Your hand is matter too, and so is the rest of your body. The chair you're sitting on is matter, and so is the air you are breathing.

The ancient Greeks were the first people to suggest that matter might be made up of many small particles they called atoms. For a long time, people believed that atoms were the smallest particles that make up matter. Today we know that atoms are actually made of even smaller particles called electrons, protons, and neutrons.

aluminum atoms mix with silicon and oxygen atoms, a gray mineral called smoky quartz forms.

Most of the time, minerals are made of a large number of atoms that have joined together to form a system of repeating units called a **crystal.** Most crystals have a regular shape and smooth, flat sides called **faces.** A crystal of quartz always has six faces.

Amethyst is one kind of quartz. Amethyst crystals form when a little bit of iron mixes with the silicon and oxygen atoms that make up pure quartz. The color of a crystal can help to identify its mineral. Amethyst is purple quartz.

# The Most Common Minerals

Quartz is not the only mineral that contains silicon and oxygen. In fact, 30 percent of all known minerals contain silicon and oxygen. These minerals, called **silicates,** are usually hard and have clear **crystals.** Feldspar, mica, hornblende, serpentine, and olivine are all common silicates.

Not all silicates are common, however. Topaz, garnet, and tourmaline contain silicon and oxygen, but they are fairly rare. Garnet is a deep red stone, while topaz is usually yellow. One kind of tourmaline is called watermelon tourmaline because it is pink on the inside and green on the outside! All three minerals are prized for their beauty and are often used in jewelry.

Like quartz, garnet crystals contain silicon and oxygen. Garnet comes in many colors, including red, brown, black, green, and yellow.

**NAME THAT MINERAL**

Serpentine is a soft, greasy, green or gray silicate mineral that forms the rock serpentinite. Both the mineral and the rock look scaly—like the skin of a serpent or snake.

Silicates make up about 90 percent of Earth's surface. They are also the main ingredient of the rocky surfaces of the Moon, Mercury, Venus, and Mars.

Even Jupiter, Saturn, Uranus, Neptune, and Pluto contain some of these minerals. Why do all the planets contain silicates? Because all the objects in our solar system formed from the same giant cloud of dust and gases about 4.6 billion years ago.

It's lucky for us that silicon is so easy to find, because it is the most important material in the microchips that run our computers. To make a silicon chip, engineers first heat quartz to separate the silicon from the oxygen. Then they grow large silicon crystals and slice them into thin wafers. Each wafer can be divided into hundreds of rectangle-shaped chips. Technicians **etch** microscopic circuit patterns onto each chip and place them in **ceramic** mounts. Did you know that a silicon chip smaller than a penny can run a personal computer?

**MICA MAGIC**

Mica (left) is an unusual mineral because it exists as black, colorless, or silvery sheets that break apart easily. Bits of ground mica are sometimes added to paint, wallpaper, decorative tiles, and Christmas tree ornaments to make them reflect light and sparkle.

# Is That a Mineral?

You shouldn't be surprised if you have trouble figuring out what people mean when they use the word *mineral*. Different people use the word in different ways.

For example, you have probably learned that when you eat a variety of healthy foods, you get all the vitamins and minerals your body needs to grow big and strong. But the "minerals" in your body are not exactly the same as the minerals in rocks. The calcium, zinc, and iron minerals that keep your blood, skin, and bones healthy are dissolved in water and do not have a repeating **crystal** structure.

A **gem** is a beautiful mineral that has been carefully cut and polished to bring out its natural

**DID YOU KNOW?**

Many **fossils,** such as the one at the right, form when "minerals" dissolved in water slowly replace an animal's bony skeleton. When the water **evaporates,** the materials arrange themselves into a crystal structure and harden to become true minerals.

10

beauty. Examples include the diamonds in engagement rings, sapphires in necklaces, and emeralds in earrings. But some of the minerals used as gemstones are unusual. The gem commonly called jade is actually two different minerals, jadeite and nephrite. Opal is made up of tiny ball-shaped grains instead of crystals. Turquoise is made up of crystals so tiny that no clear pattern can be seen.

Even though oil is mined from deep underground, it exists as a liquid, so it is not a mineral. Sand isn't a mineral either, because it doesn't always have the same chemical makeup. The black sand beaches of Hawaii, Scotland, and Greece are made up of tiny pieces of hardened lava. The pure white sand beaches of the Philippine Islands are made of bits of broken seashells.

The diamonds and sapphire in this necklace have been carefully cut and polished. Most sapphires are blue, but they may also be pink, green, violet, gray, or yellow.

## IMAGINE THAT!

Have you ever noticed a hard white or light brown material slowly building up along the inside edges of a clay flowerpot? That material is made up of minerals that have dissolved out of water. People sometimes refer to drinking water that contains a lot of dissolved minerals as "hard water." Drinking water with just a few dissolved minerals is called "soft water."

# Below the Surface

Just like a birthday cake, Earth is made up of layers. Our planet's top layer—the one you walk on every day—is called the **crust.** Like the icing on a cake, it is thin compared to the layers below it.

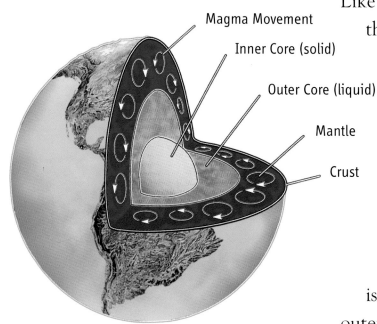

Magma Movement

Inner Core (solid)

Outer Core (liquid)

Mantle

Crust

The thin outer layer of Earth is the crust. The next layer, the mantle, is made of magma that is constantly moving. The core is made of an outer liquid core and an inner solid core.

Just below Earth's crust is a thicker layer called the **mantle.** The mantle is made of hot, liquid rock called **magma.** Earth's innermost layer is called the **core.** The outer part of the core is liquid, while the inner part is solid. Both parts of the core are made of metals—iron and nickel. All metals are **elements** that can combine to form minerals. Iron is one of the elements found in the minerals pyrite, magnetite, and marcasite.

Earth's inner core is sizzling hot—over 9,000 degrees Fahrenheit (5,000 degrees Celsius). Heat energy from the core naturally tries to escape to a cooler place. As the heat moves upward, magma at the bottom of the mantle is carried toward Earth's surface. At the same time, cooler magma at the top of the mantle moves down to take its place. Over millions of years, magma circles slowly through the mantle.

Sometimes magma at the top of the mantle is forced into cracks in Earth's crust and spills out onto the surface. Magma that blasts out of an erupting **volcano** is called lava. When lava cools, it forms the tiny **crystals** of feldspar, olivine, pyroxene, and other minerals found in some kinds of **igneous rock.** Igneous rocks with large crystals form from magma that cools slowly deep underground.

Kilauea, the most active volcano in the world, is located on the southeastern slope of Mauna Loa in Hawaii Volcanoes National Park. Each time it erupts, fiery hot lava flows over the land, destroying everything in its path.

# What Mineral Is That?

When you walk down the street, it is easy for you to tell the difference between friends and strangers. To pick a friend out of a crowd, all you have to do is pay close attention to the way people look and how they act.

Kaolinite is a soft mineral. It is used to make clay, coatings for paper, and filler for rubber tires.

Scientists do the same thing when they try to identify minerals. They study a mineral's **properties**—the way it looks and how it acts. For example, scientists look at a mineral's color and its shininess. They also examine the mineral's form and **crystal** structure. Next, scientists test the mineral's hardness and observe how it breaks. They may even use their senses of smell, touch, and taste to identify minerals.

Kaolinite is a soft, white mineral that smells like dirt. Some people use it to make pottery. Talc feels greasy, and it is so soft that you can break it apart with your fingers. Halite, or table salt, is a mineral you taste just about every day. *But some minerals are very poisonous. You should never taste a mineral unless a teacher or scientist has said it is safe to do so.*

**DID YOU KNOW?**

A mineralogist is a scientist who studies the properties of minerals in order to identify and classify them.

14

Like a scientist, you can study the properties of the minerals in a rock. Look closely to examine a specimen's color, shininess, form, and hardness.

In many cases, you can easily observe and test a mineral the same way a scientist does. To give this a try, read the next few pages of this book carefully. Another good way to identify a mineral sample is to get a field guide to rocks and minerals from your local library. Then you can study the photographs and read the descriptions. These books include the most common minerals and may even have maps that show you where rocks and minerals are most likely to be found.

**BLAST FROM THE PAST**

A German scientist named Georgius Agricola was one of the first people to study and compare the properties of different minerals. In 1546, he wrote a book describing the color, the shininess, and the hardness of minerals commonly found near his home.

# Taking a Good, Long Look

Several different minerals may be found in the same rock. In this sample, you can easily see blue azurite crystals and green malachite crystals.

When scientists find a mineral, the first thing they do is look at it very carefully. You can do the same thing. Begin by looking at the color of the **crystals.** Scientists know that malachite crystals are always green, and azurite crystals are always blue. But the color of a crystal isn't always enough to identify a mineral. After all, diamond crystals can be colorless, yellow, blue, or even red. Topaz is usually yellow, but it can also be colorless, blue, pink, or orange.

Next, examine the arrangement of the crystals that make up the mineral. Sometimes this can provide clues to the mineral's identity. Crystals of selenite, gypsum, aragonite, and staurolite sometimes form at right angles, creating a cross-shaped mineral. In fact, the name *staurolite* comes from the Greek word *stauros*, meaning "cross."

**DID YOU KNOW?**

Many people call the pointy writing tip of a pencil its "lead," but that gray material is not really lead. It is made of the mineral graphite, that consists of only carbon atoms.

16

Now look at the number, shape, and location of the crystal's **faces.** A quartz crystal always has six faces and is shaped like a hexagon. Beryl and graphite crystals are also shaped like hexagons. Crystals of halite and galena have six faces and are shaped like cubes.

Cube-shaped galena crystals are mixed with sphalerite in this mineral sample. Galena is a major source of lead, while sphalerite is an important source of zinc.

A mineral's shininess can also help you identify it. Metals such as gold, copper, silver, and platinum reflect light well, so they always look shiny. Nonmetals do not reflect light. They absorb it. That is why quartz, sulfur, talc, and cinnabar look dull.

Finally, take a look at the mineral's form. Gold can come in flakes or nuggets, asbestos comes in long fibers, and mica comes in thin, flat sheets.

**IMAGINE THAT!**

Beryl is a colorless mineral made of beryllium, aluminum, silicon, and oxygen atoms. When just a few chromium atoms are mixed in, the mineral turns green, and we call it emerald.

# Let's Get Physical

Sometimes just looking at a mineral won't give you all the information you need to identify it. That's when it's time to try a few experiments.

One of the easiest experiments is a streak test. Some minerals leave behind a streak of color when you rub them against an unglazed white porcelain tile. A mineral's streak color is not always the same as the color of its **crystals.** For example, a brick red mineral called hematite makes a brown streak. Chalcopyrite is a golden yellow mineral, but it leaves behind a greenish black streak.

Even though hematite is brick red, it leaves behind a brown streak. It contains **atoms** of iron and oxygen.

Because a mineral always has the same crystal structure, it always breaks in the same way. For example, mica always breaks into thin sheets.

### DID YOU KNOW?

Sometimes scientists can identify a mineral by weighing it. Shiny metallic minerals, such as copper, usually weigh more than dull nonmetals, such as talc. If you have equal-sized samples of copper and talc, the copper sample will be heavier. Gold is one of the heaviest minerals in the world.

Diamond breaks in four directions and forms smaller crystals shaped like pyramids. Some other minerals do not break into pieces with easily recognized shapes. Quartz is a good example. *If you decide to try tapping a mineral with a small hammer, be sure that an adult is present and that you are wearing safety glasses. You can try this test on a mineral sample from your backyard or a local park, but don't try it on a piece of jewelry.*

Some minerals have special properties that make them easy to identify. For example, a mineral known as magnetite is magnetic—it attracts other metals. Fluorite is easy to identify because ultraviolet light makes it fluoresce, or glow in the dark. When you toss a small piece of calcite into a glass of vinegar, the mixture will start to bubble as the acid in the vinegar reacts with the calcite.

## WHAT AN INVENTION!

About 2,800 years ago, people living in China noticed that one end of a rock containing magnetite always points north. Chinese sailors realized that they could use this special property to help them find their way across stormy seas. Then Chinese soldiers began using magnetite to find the best routes around tall mountains and across blazing-hot deserts. This is how the compass was invented.

When you shine ultraviolet light on fluorite, it seems to glow in the dark. In its purest form, fluorite is colorless.

# How Hard Is That Mineral?

Sometimes the easiest way to identify a mineral is by scratching it. In 1822, a German scientist named Friedrich Mohs invented a simple scale for comparing the hardnesses of different minerals. It was such a good system that scientists still use Mohs scale today. You can use it too!

Talc is so soft that it is number one on the Mohs scale. Talc is used to make crayons, paint, paper, and soap.

All minerals fall somewhere along the Mohs scale. It lists the hardnesses of ten common minerals. Minerals with low numbers are soft and easy to scratch. Talc is so soft that it is used to make baby powder. Minerals with high numbers are very hard and difficult to scratch. The only thing hard enough to scratch a diamond is another diamond.

Gold, copper, and silver are all fairly soft minerals. Each one has a Mohs number of 2H to 3. The

Mohs number for magnetite is 6, while olivine is 7, and a sapphire rates 9.

The Mohs scale is not an even scale. In other words, diamond is not ten times harder than talc. Actually, diamond—the hardest mineral—is 150 times harder than corundum—the second-hardest mineral on the Mohs scale.

## MOHS' SCALE

| MOHS' NUMBER | MINERAL | DESCRIPTION OF HARDNESS |
| --- | --- | --- |
| 1 | Talc | Can be scratched by a fingernail. |
| 2 | Gypsum | Can be scratched by a fingernail. |
| 3 | Calcite | Can be scratched by a copper penny. |
| 4 | Fluorite | Can be scratched by glass. |
| 5 | Apatite | Can be scratched by a steel knife. |
| 6 | Feldspar | Can be scratched by a steel knife. |
| 7 | Quartz | Can be scratched by sandpaper. |
| 8 | Topaz | Can be scratched by an emery board. |
| 9 | Corundum | Can be scratched by a diamond. |
| 10 | Diamond | Can be scratched only by another diamond. |

# Digging Up Minerals

Wherever you see rocks, there are minerals. Minerals are found in mountains, on beaches, and even under your feet. Many of the minerals that people consider most valuable are mined. These include diamond, gold, topaz, and copper.

Copper ores can often be found close to Earth's surface. This copper mine in New Mexico is an open-pit mine, meaning that ore is mined on the surface, not in deep, underground shafts.

People also mine minerals for the metals they contain. An **ore** is any mineral that contains enough metal to be mined profitably. After ores are mined, they are usually crushed into powder, and some of the waste rock is separated out. Then the metal is removed from the remaining powder by heating and melting it, "zapping" it with electricity, or adding chemicals to the sample.

## BLAST FROM THE PAST

About 7,000 years ago, people living in what is now Europe began digging copper out of the ground and using it to make jewelry, tools, and weapons. About 5,000 years ago, they started mixing copper with tin to make bronze. Bronze is harder and stronger than copper. The period when bronze was widely used is known as the Bronze Age.

The melting process, known as smelting, is commonly used to separate iron from hematite or magnetite. It takes place in a blast furnace that can heat the rock to more than 2,900 degrees Fahrenheit (1,600 degrees Celsius). An electrical current can be used to separate aluminum from bauxite ore. When special chemicals are added to azurite or malachite, most of the ore dissolves, leaving pure copper metal behind.

Each year, millions of tons of ore are smelted to purify iron. Then the iron can be used to make steel, sheet metal, or electromagnets.

## ORES CONTAINING MINERALS

| ORE | METAL |
| --- | --- |
| Azurite, bornite, chalcocite, chalcopyrite, cuprite, malachite | Copper |
| Bauxite | Aluminum |
| Cassiterite | Tin |
| Chromite | Chromium |
| Cinnabar | Mercury |
| Galena | Lead |
| Hematite, magnetite, marcasite, siderite, pyrite | Iron |
| Ilmenite, rutile | Titanium |
| Magnesite | Magnesium |
| Pitchblende | Uranium |
| Sphalerite | Zinc |

# How People Use Minerals

What do mirrors, radios, computers, cars, roads, jewelry, clothes, and toothpaste have in common? They are all made from minerals. In fact, it is almost impossible to think of any product that doesn't contain minerals.

The SPARTAN research satellite is one of many spacecraft covered with gold foil. The gold protects the spacecraft from harmful cosmic rays.

Gold, silver, platinum, and diamonds are made into jewelry. But these minerals also have other important uses. Photographic film wouldn't work without silver. Platinum is used to make antipollution devices for cars. About 80 percent of all the diamonds dug out of the ground are used to make industrial cutting equipment. Why are diamonds so good for cutting? Because nothing is harder than a diamond!

**DID YOU KNOW?**

When the mineral gypsum is heated, it forms a fine powder called plaster of paris. If this material is mixed with water, it can be used to make **ceramics,** models, and statues. Many dentists use plaster of paris to make casts of people's teeth.

Aluminum is strong, lightweight, and does not rust. It is perfect for making bicycles, soda cans, cars, and power lines. Stainless-steel objects are made from chromium, a metal that comes from chromite **ore.** Magnetite is used to make magnets for compasses, refrigera-

tor doors, and industrial machinery. The uranium from pitchblende generates electricity for lights, televisions, toasters, hair dryers, blenders, and coffee makers in homes all over the world.

Fluorite is the main source of the fluoride added to toothpaste and drinking water. It helps keep our teeth strong and healthy. Titanium is so tough and strong that it is used to build airplanes and spacecraft. It may also be used to color paper, paint, and plastics white. Sulfur is used to make chemicals that kill insects and to make fertilizers that help plants grow. Halite is the table salt that flavors our food, and borax helps to keep our clothes clean and fresh.

These soda cans are made of aluminum. Aluminum does not rust because it forms a protective layer of aluminum oxide when it is exposed to the air.

**THAT'S INCREDIBLE!**

It takes thirty-five different minerals just to make a television set, and more than thirty-two to build and operate even the simplest computer.

# Amazing Minerals

Have you ever dreamed about finding the biggest diamond or gold nugget in the world? That would be very exciting, and selling it would certainly make you rich.

The Royal Scepter of England contains the Star of Africa diamond. It is the largest cut diamond in the world.

Believe it or not, in 1905, a 1.4-pound (0.6-kilogram) diamond was discovered in Cullinan, South Africa. It was cut into nine large jewels and ninety-six smaller ones. The largest **gem** was named the Star of Africa. It became part of the British Royal Scepter and is now on display at the Tower of London in London, England.

In 1869, the world's biggest gold nugget was found in Moliagul in Victoria, Australia. It weighs 156 pounds (71 kilograms). The largest topaz, discovered in Brazil in 1940, weighs 596 pounds (271 kilograms) and can be seen at the American Museum of Natural History in New York City.

People have also found some pretty amazing mineral formations deep inside caves. When the mineral-rich waters that flow through caves **evaporate,** long, icicle-shaped stalactites sometimes grow down from the ceiling. In some caves, thick, stubby stalagmites rise up from the floor. Stalagmites often grow more than 50 feet (15 meters) high and 33 feet (10 meters) across. They usually have broad, rounded tips.

Some caves also have beautiful "flowers" and "pearls" made of calcite or gypsum along the walls. Delicate mineral "drapes" may even hang from the ceiling. Some are so thin that a person can see right through them. All these structures consist of minerals that once made up the layers of limestone that dissolved to form the cave.

Grotte du Maire is a cave in Herault, France. It features stunning stalactites and stalagmites.

## EXPLAIN THAT NAME!

Have you ever wondered how the San Francisco 49ers football team got its name? The story began in 1848, when a man named James Wilson Marshall found flakes of gold in a stream near what is now Sacramento, California. During the next year, over 100,000 people—known as "forty-niners" because of the year—came to California with dreams of getting rich. That is how the state was settled.

# Be a Mineral Collector

Now that you know a little bit about minerals and how to identify them, you might want to try collecting some. You can buy minerals at many kinds of stores or at a local mineral show. You can also view them at a natural history museum, but it might be more fun to hunt for them in rocks at a local park, in a field, or in the woods.

Before you plan your first mineral collecting trip, you will need to gather a few pieces of equipment. You will also need to learn a few rules. When you bring the minerals or mineral-filled rocks home, you can try some of the tests described in this book.

You can learn a great deal by examining the rock and mineral collection at a large museum. This collection is housed at Harvard University in Boston, Massachusetts.

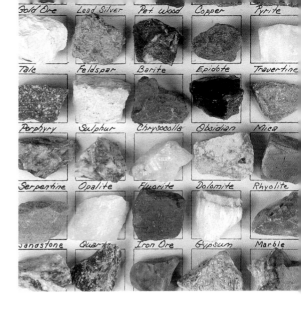

Once you have identified the minerals, you may want to create a system for labeling, organizing, and storing them. Then you will always be able to find a particular sample later. You can arrange your specimens any way you like—by color, by **crystal** shape, by collection site, or even alphabetically. As your collection grows, being organized becomes more and more important.

This neatly organized personal rock collection is arranged by location. You can start your own collection by gluing specimens to cardboard or placing them in a box with compartments.

## COLOSSAL COLLECTION

One of the largest and most interesting mineral collections in the world is on display at the National Museum of Natural History in Paris, France. The collection was started by King Louis XIII of France in the early 1600s.

## WHAT YOU NEED

- Hiking boots
- A map and compass
- A pick and rock hammer to collect samples
- Safety glasses to keep rock chips out of your eyes
- A small paintbrush to remove dirt and extra rock from samples
- A camera to take photographs of rock formations
- A hand lens to get an up-close look at minerals
- A notebook for recording when and where you find each mineral
- A field guide to rocks and minerals

## WHAT YOU NEED TO KNOW

- Never go mineral collecting alone. Go with a group that includes an adult.
- Know how to read a map and use a compass.
- Always get a landowner's permission before walking on private property. If you find some interesting minerals, ask the owner if you may remove them.
- Before removing samples from public land, make sure mineral collecting is allowed. Many natural rock formations are protected by law.
- Respect nature. Do not disturb living things, and do not litter.

# Glossary

**atom**: smallest unit of an element that still has all the properties of the element

**ceramic**: made of clay

**core**: center of Earth. The inner core is solid, and the outer core is liquid.

**crust**: outer layer of Earth

**crystal**: repeating structural unit within most minerals

**element**: substance that contains only one kind of atom

**etch**: to engrave or draw on metal or glass

**evaporate**: to change from a liquid to a gas

**face**: smooth, flat side of a crystal

**fossil**: remains or evidence of ancient life

**gem**: beautiful mineral that has been cut and polished

**igneous rock**: kind of rock that forms when magma from Earth's mantle cools and hardens

**magma**: hot, soft rock that makes up Earth's mantle. When magma spills out onto Earth's surface, it is called lava.

**mantle**: layer of Earth between the crust and outer core. It is made of soft rock called magma.

**matter**: anything that takes up space as a solid, liquid, or gas

**ore**: mineral that contains enough metal to be mined profitably

**property**: trait or characteristic that helps make identification possible

**silicate**: mineral that contains silicon and oxygen

**volcano**: crack in Earth's surface that extends into the mantle, and from which comes melted rock

# To Find Out More

## BOOKS

Blobaum, Cindy. *Geology Rocks!: 50 Hands-On Activities to Explore the Earth.* Charlotte, Vt.: Williamson, 1999.

Downs, Sandra. *Earth's Hidden Treasures.* Brookfield, Conn.: Twenty First Century Books, 1999.

Kittinger, Jo S. *A Look at Minerals: From Galena to Gold.* Danbury, Conn.: Franklin Watts, 1998.

Oldershaw, Cally. *3D-Eyewitness: Rocks and Minerals.* New York: Dorling Kindersley, 1999.

Pellant, Chris. *The Best Book of Fossils, Rocks, and Minerals.* New York: Kingfisher, 2000.

Pellant, Chris. *Collecting Gems & Minerals: Hold the Treasures of the Earth in the Palm of Your Hand.* New York: Sterling, 1998.

Ricciuti, Edward, and Margaret W. Carruthers. *National Audubon Society First Field Guide to Rocks and Minerals.* New York: Scholastic, 1998.

Staedter, Tracy. *Rocks and Minerals.* Pleasantville, N.Y.: Reader's Digest, 1999.

Symes R. F. *Crystals and Gems.* New York: Dorling Kindersley, 2000.

## ORGANIZATIONS

**Geological Survey of Canada**
601 Booth Street
Ottawa, Ontario
KIA 0E8
613/995-3084

**U.S. Geological Survey (USGS)**
507 National Center
12201 Sunrise Valley Drive
Reston, VA 22092
703/648-4748

# Index

*Italicized* page numbers indicate illustrations.

Agricola Georgius, 15
aluminum 6, 7, 17, 23, 24-25, *25*
amethyst 6, 7, *7*
apatite 21, *21*
aragonite 16
asbestos 17
atoms 6-7, 18
Australia 26
azurite 16, *16*, 23

bauxite 23
beryl 17
beryllium 17
borax 25
Brazil 27
British royal scepter 26, *26*
bronze 22
Bronze Age 22

calcite 4, 5, 19, 21, 27
calcium 6, 10
caves 27
chalcopyrite 18
chromium 17, 25
cinnabar 17
computer chips 9
copper 17, 18, 20, 22
core 12, *12*
corundum 21
crust 12, *12*, 13
crystals 7, 13, 16-17, 18, 19, 29

diamonds 4, 11, *11*, 16, 19, 20, 21, 22, 24, 26, *26*
dolomite 5

elements 6
emeralds 11, 17

faces 7
feldspar 5, 8, 13, 21
field guides 15, 29
fluorite 19, *19*, 21, 25
49ers 27
fossils 10, *10*

galena 17, *17*
garnet 8, *8*
gems 10-11, 26
gold 4, *4*, 17, 18, 20, 22, 24, *24*, 26, 27
granite 5, *5*, 6
graphite 16, 17, 23
gypsum 16, 21, 24, 27

halite 14, 17, 25
"hard water" 11
hematite 18, *18*, 23
hornblende 8

igneous rock 13
iron 6, 10, 12, 18, 23, *23*

jade 11

kaolinite 14, *14*

lava 11, 13, *13*
limestone 27

magma 12-13
magnesium 6
magnetite 12, 19, 21, 23, 25
malachite 16, *16*, 23
mantle 12, *12*, 13
marble 5

marcasite 12
Marshall, James Wilson 27
matter 7
mica 5, 8, 9, 17, 18
mineral collecting 28-29, *28*, *29*
mineralogists 14
mining 22, *22*, 23
Mohs, Friedrich 20
Mohs' scale 20-21
Moon 8

nickel 12
nutritional minerals 10, 21

oil 11
olivine 8, 13, 21
opal 11
ore 22-23, *23*, 25
oxygen 6-7, 8, 9, 17

peridot 13
pitchblende 25
planets 8-9
plaster of paris 24
platinum 17, 24
potassium 6
properties 4, 14, 15, 16-17, 18-19
pyrite 12
pyroxene 13

quartz 4, 5, 6-7, *6*, 8, 9, 17, 19, 21

rocks 4, 5, 6, 15, 22, 28, 29

sand 11
sandstone 6
sapphire 11, *11*, 21
selenite 16
serpentine 8
serpentinite 8
shapes 17
shininess 17
silicates 8-9
silicon 6-7, 8-9, 17
silver 17, 20, 24
slate 6
smelting 23, *23*
smoky quartz 7
sodium 6
"soft water" 11
South Africa 26
stalactites 27, *27*
stalagmites 27, *27*
Star of Africa diamond 26, *26*
staurolite 16
streak test 18
structure 4-5, 14, 18
sulfur 17, 25

talc 4, 14, 17, 18, 20, *20*, 21
tin 22
titanium 25
topaz 8, 16, 21, 22, 26-27
tourmaline 8
turquoise 11

uranium 25

volcanoes 13, *13*

watermelon tourmaline 8

zinc 10